OUT OF OFFICE

IMAGES BY A TRAVELLING SALESMAN

Xmas 2009

Jack Delmonte

OUT OF OFFICE

IMAGES BY A TRAVELLING SALESMAN

To Sue ~ Neil

Best Regards

[signature]

h::thivebooks

For Hetty and Ernie

Out of Office – images by a travelling salesman

© Text and images: Jack Delmonte.

ISBN: 978-1-906316-29-7

Published in 2009 by HotHive Books, Evesham, UK.
www.thehothive.com

Printed in Great Britain by BAS Printers, Wiltshire, UK.

Frontispiece: Spain, 2008

Opposite: Beijing, 2008

Overleaf: Dubai, 2008

Contents

8   Introduction

10 **The kick off**

12 **Trying not to get mugged!**

14 **A Malvinas moment**

18 **Childhood memories**

20 **The five man car wash**

22 **Not as good for business as it first appears**

26 **Intellectual rights**

30 **A strange, modern place**

32 **A lovely place to have lunch but not to do business**

36 **Business, pleasure and a typhoon**

44 **Peace and the temple**

48 **The Basque connection**

54 **Designer frenzy**

56 **It seemed like a good idea at the time**

60 **A quick visit**

62 **Home base**

63 Print ordering

I am currently out of office

Thank you for contacting me. I am currently travelling overseas, so do not have easy access to emails, cannot digest my food properly and due to constant flying, I am perpetually jetlagged. If you have any cures for the above or have business with a decent budget and a need for an IT security vendor, then please contact me on the following number; if not, then leave a message.

Foreword

What has forever struck me about Jack since we first met many years ago is the feeling that he has always been searching for himself; being brave enough and bold enough to take the tough decisions without hesitating to break out from the pack in the process.

He has spent his life being a rule breaker. Sometimes it has worked in his favour, sometimes to his detriment, but he has never needed encouragement or applause to keep moving on and keep trying new things.

So when Jack told me about this book, it summed him up in an instant.

Sales is in his blood and his personality is such that he has always found himself in the most unusual of situations, meeting the most beautiful of people.

He is forever travelling the world and his gregarious, curious nature means he spots the hidden treasures and unusual opportunities that pass most people by.

This, even more than his brilliant business mind, is his defining gift; a boundless creativity and an insatiable appetite for new experiences, with his alter-ego photography career showcasing what really drives him.

Jack's book combines his two talents, capturing in the process the art of just 'getting up and doing it'.

Whilst so many ponder the reasons for not giving things a go, the sumptuous photographs and witty vignettes in this book show what can happen if you actually do.

It is life through the eyes of someone who has travelled the world with a smile on his face and the confidence of being good at telling stories and even better at closing deals. For Jack, life's a pitch.

Enjoy the journey.

René Carayol
Business guru and leading business speaker

Introduction

I gazed out of the window, straining to see the beautiful wastes of Greenland below as my new acquaintance, another technology salesman seated next to me, explained his employment tactics. "I always hit 104%; nothing more, nothing less. Always manage 104%. This way they cannot fire me for underperforming and they don't promote me because I am too boring. It works, I tell you. I am the invisible salesman who makes enough but never gets threatened with redundancies when times are tough. How about you, what do you do to keep your job?"

We had been talking for about fifteen minutes and it had been the wrong fifteen minutes. I always aim to open a conversation, if I must open one, when the landing procedure has started. That way, if the contact is interesting, there is just enough time to exchange business cards without getting too personal.

What me? What do I do? I thought about it for a few seconds. "Well," I said, "I always do too much, get the accolades, get the promotion and eventually get made redundant when the company is sold, or when politics get in the way and they have had enough of me."

"Well," he replied, "sounds all too exciting for me."

Yes, *so* exciting, I thought as we headed to Boston for the management meeting to determine our business plans for 2008. A meeting that was to cover a recently announced corporate strategy where the decision had been made to sell off the division I worked in. The sell-off was targeted to be completed in the first six months of 2008. So I knew we had a horizon of around six months for things to get well and truly exciting before I had a potential redundancy situation.

My business division is a part of a large US-based,

high-tech internet security enterprise. In the main, my business aims to outsource the security of an enterprise network, thereby protecting the network perimeter and the devices that manage it (such as the firewall) and tracking any potential intruders.

We sell directly to enterprises, end users or we go through business partners, who resell or franchise our services. The products and solutions are then managed remotely from our base in the States or, in the case of some international partners, they franchise the management of the service. This is particularly useful in countries where sharing potentially sensitive information with an American based company is not politically palatable and where local language skills are useful, such as China and parts of Latin America.

So, it seemed like the job would end soon and I had an idea for a project that would make use of the time left. This was to document my situation in a book with images and words that would explain what I really do and where I go to do it. Now the question was, could I get the time to take the pictures for this whilst performing to my company's professional standards and expectations? And how and where was I going to be able to complete the project?

We were destined to be sold off (or 'divested' in business parlance) and we needed to maintain the company's sales efforts. We also needed to keep the partners informed of the divestiture and, as I had a large role in these communication efforts, my normal patch was extended from Europe, the Middle East and Africa to the entire globe. Working for a US company based in London, I was designated as Global Channels Director, managing international business partners. Now that's unusual, very unusual – most US companies like to use US-based staff for this function.

So in my bag, for the first time on my business travels, was my small compact Leica rangefinder film camera (later replaced by a digital Leica), one lens and a handful of fresh 35mm black and white film canisters. My objective was to take as many pictures as possible in the short time I had; images that could depict the business traveller's world I live in and maybe, just maybe, produce some images that could help tell a story – a story of a travelling salesman.

The kick off
San Jose, USA

With the excitement of my new project in tow, I flew to the company Sales Conference Kick Off event in San Jose, California. My time was interspersed between a hotel room, meeting rooms and the bar. I did not manage to take my camera out once during the conference. So here was the challenge, I had to be committed to my paid job first and the photography project had to come second.

On the day before we flew back to the UK, a couple of us decided to drive off into the hills and we found ourselves in a funky Los Gatos bar. For the first time that week, we all had a chance to relax.

I raised my camera as the guitarist tuned up and as he kicked off his gig my photographic adventure began.

Trying not to get mugged!
Sao Paulo, Brazil

Before going to Sao Paulo for the first time, I had a pre-flight conversation with 'my guy' in town. "When you get to the airport follow these instructions," he said. "Look for the hotel driver and when you see your name on a board do not approach the driver and announce yourself, but look around to see if your name appears on other drivers' boards first. If your name appears on more than one board, then phone the hotel and check out the driver's name and car registration number. This process is necessary as sometimes the hotel 'leaks out' some executive pick-up details and a 'dummy driver' is sent out and a potential kidnapping can occur."

I commented during this conversation that this seemed slightly paranoid, but then he told me that one of our local Sao Paulo employees had been kidnapped recently when going to his car in the office underground car park. He had been taken by two guys at gun point, driven to a *favela* (slum area) and held there whilst his bank cards were used to empty his account in a 'midnight run'. A midnight run is where the credit cards are used just before and just after midnight to achieve maximum takings by circumventing the daily cash withdrawal limit.

I approached the airport terminal exit carrying my suitcase, briefcase and camera, scanning the area for my hotel driver, but I could not see him anywhere. After some twenty minutes of being hassled by taxi touts, I decided to head for the taxi rank and the stand where you pre-pay.

I eventually arrived at my hotel after a few hours of manoeuvring the Sao Paulo traffic and received an apology that the hotel had mislaid my request for an airport car.

Later, I met our local representative and was told to carry nothing of value outside the hotel: no watch, camera or wallet. He instructed me to carry just a one hundred dollar bill in my pocket because if I was mugged it was best to have something to give them. "Call it a mugger's tax if you like, we do." He said to also carry a $20 bill in my sock for the post-mugging taxi ride home!

After various meetings with local business partners and wonderful evenings spent savouring the night life, the camera had barely seen the light of day, nor night. Here was I, putting the job as my first priority, at the same time as being in a hostile street environment and subject to tight time constraints. I started to wonder if this project was going to be just too difficult.

This first trip to Sao Paulo made me realise that working in Latin America was going to be very much like my Spanish and Italian experiences. Your business partners need to know you well before deeper relationships can be formed. In Northern Europe, for example, a short meeting can lead to big things. However, in Latin America, long meetings have to happen first, with accompanying long lunches and dinners. I also had to slow down my London cockney accent, as the partners were used to working with Americans and spoke American English. From Sao Paulo I headed to Buenos Aires for a one-day stopover, visiting a potential business partner.

A Malvinas moment
Buenos Aires, Argentina

I arrived in this beautiful city late in the evening with only one meeting booked for the next day. This left me with at least two hours of free time in the afternoon, before heading back out to the airport for a short flight to Chile.

The meeting was over by lunchtime and I had a few precious hours before I had to be back at the airport. The hotel was situated on the Plaza San Martin, one of the main green areas in the city. It was quite still and peaceful in the Plaza, quite unlike horrendously busy Sao Paulo.

Walking across the Plaza, I could see what looked like bayonets on top of two rifles, moving back and forth, poking above the top of a high wall. I was drawn to the scene and having arrived there was faced with two female soldiers holding guns, marching to and fro in front of a monument. The monument had hundreds of names etched across its stone frontage. The soldiers glanced at me, I smiled and they smiled back.

Just then, a woman approached and placed flowers at the base of the memorial. It was not until then that I actually realised what I was looking at. The lettering on the top identified it as the Argentina memorial to the Malvinas War (or Falklands War as it's known to the British). I remember that war: it was known as 'Thatcher's War' and was the catalyst for her resurgence of popularity in the early 1980s. What I did not know was the large number of lives lost by the Argentinians. It was a deeply moving and humbling moment.

Just as dusk settled in the park, I headed back to the hotel. On the way, I passed a fountain where young people were entwined around each other in an atmosphere of calm and happiness. I took a few shots and headed back to the room to pick up my luggage. As I sat on the hotel bed, a shaft of light came through the window, hitting the chair and table opposite me. I picked up my camera and clicked off a few more shots. At last I was capturing images and enjoying it.

Childhood memories
Santiago, Chile

Santiago, Chile has been a long held fascination for me since my school days. At junior school, there was a Chilean boy in our class. One day after school we looked at my treasured possession, the *Book of World Flags*. He described Chile as a magical kingdom with the sea on one side and the mountains on the other, where huge birds and whales lived. The image of Chile he portrayed has stayed with me ever since.

Imagining Santiago, I had always envisaged an old colonial city with Spanish architecture and that amazing backdrop of the Andes Mountains my childhood friend had described. What I found instead was a mini-Beijing. Cranes and building works were everywhere. A spurt of growth has propelled Chile into a relative powerhouse in Latin American terms.

The scheduled meeting was with a potential major partner in the country and proved to be interesting as they explained their business expansion plans for Peru and Columbia. We discussed the 'new Latin economies' and the business landscape. The meeting could have been anywhere in Europe.

As I walked away from their offices, I witnessed three window washers suspended high up on a new office block, their buckets swaying in the breeze. The cleaning seemed a long and fruitless task as building dust swirled around the area, falling across the newly cleaned glass.

The five man car wash
Mexico City, Mexico

The flight from Chile via Sao Paulo back to Mexico was long and arduous. I arrived at Mexico City just before 5:30am and headed through customs. This entailed long queues and baggage being continually x-rayed. I was worried about my film being overly scanned; more than three times may fog a film of the speed I was using. But customs refused to hand examine the film canisters separately so the film was x-rayed for the fourth time this trip.

I arrived at the hotel in time for a quick freshen up and then headed up to the hotel's executive floor dining area for the business meeting with our partner in Mexico. I had not foreseen any chance of getting the camera out, but during the conversation we discovered a shared love of photography and I asked if he would mind me capturing a record of the table where we had just met. He said sure. "The English never cease to amuse me – such eccentrics!" On arriving back at the amazing new airport terminal building, I photographed the interior of that as well, despite being interrupted by airport security. I pleaded to retain my film with the excuse that I am, after all just a "harmless English eccentric".

One thing stuck in my mind on the flight home. On the way to the hotel, our taxi stopped at a junction for a red light. (A taxi stopping at a red light is in itself a seemingly major feat in Mexico City!) The car in front was pounced on by five guys, who not only washed the windscreen, as you can witness traffic light car window washers performing in most big cities, but they washed the whole car in the time it took for the lights to change. They used buckets, washing leathers and even wax. It was an amazing job, all done in a few minutes.

When they finished one of the men held his hand out towards the driver's window but the spotless car drove off. Nothing was given, nothing was exchanged but a few glances and the car washers moved back to the pavement looking dejected. I asked my driver how much money each of these guys expected to earn everyday doing this. "Oh a dollar on a good day when they are lucky – but often they are unlucky."

Not as good for business as it first appears

Sydney, Australia

Australia, regardless of being a large country geographically, does appear to be a small country with minimal opportunities from a business perspective. And worse, there is a lot of competition, as technology companies utilise the region's enormous geography and local skills as a test bed for new products and innovations. In addition, you have the close proximity to Australia's biggest markets of China and Japan.

I stayed in the old GPO building, now the Westin Hotel on Sydney's Martin Place. The hotel consists of a Victorian mall surrounded by classical buildings, including the 1927 World War I War Memorial Cenetaph still adorned with wreaths from the recent ANZAC day. It's a very popular place, crowded with office workers and dispatch riders on their lunch break, all being entertained by buskers in front of the newly placed, tall Christmas tree.

Inside the hotel, beautiful late afternoon light streamed through the windows into restored corridors and stairwells enhancing its early 20th-century structure.

24

Intellectual rights
Beijing, China

I was in Beijing negotiating a partner contract with a major technology business. The business was government owned, as all major indigenous technology businesses are in China. There was some concern about the technology transfer element of the contract. This was especially prevalent when we discussed the translation of our US English operational manual into Mandarin, which we wanted the client to fund, as this was a costly process.

The very young and bright lawyer on their side of the table insisted that if they paid for the translation, they owned the manual and its contents. After much debate, it appeared that the 'contents' meant the intellectual property element of the manual and not just the instructional areas. This can be a very difficult situation. You want the business and you need to expand your operations into this high growth region; but you know that all those years of research, development and operational experience can be signed away in a stroke of a pen – if you are not diligent.

While I was in Beijing, one of my team was gracious enough to take me on a day tour of the city and its environs. The city feels like it is literally growing under your feet, with the constant pounding of pile drivers for building foundations and cranes everywhere. It was also the year of the Beijing Olympics, bringing with it even more building activity than normal.

The choked new freeways fuel the city's already heavy pollution. All but a relatively small number of old housing quarters have been demolished, with those remaining being rejuvenated as showpieces for the Olympics. These

hutong (alleyway) houses are now in great demand for their space and traditional history.

We visited Beihai Park, which is an old imperial garden dating from the 10th century. It contains numerous historically important structures, palaces and temples. A lake with pavilions around its perimeter covers more than half of the park. In the pavilions, couples danced to live music or portable music players. Apparently they dance here because they have little room at home. However, it

seemed more like a chance to show off their dancing skills to me!

At my request, we also visited '798 Art Zone', which is a thriving artist community. Situated in a fifty-year-old decommissioned military factory complex, it has buildings of differing style and stages of re-gentrification. Within the complex, art lives in the various galleries and also in the streets, where sculptures point to their industrial past.

A strange, modern place
Dubai, UAE

The last time I was in Dubai was on a stopover heading back from a visit to Australia. The year was 1978. It's changed a bit since then!

First, the small tea stall that used to be behind the customs shed has gone and so has the camel owner outside the terminal offering tourist stopover photo opportunities. There are a lot more hotels to choose from than the solitary Intercontinental that offered the only accommodation when I was last there. In fact, as widely documented, the place has gone a bit mad. The first evidence of this is as you fly in and see the tip of the soon-to-be world's tallest building, the Burj Dubai, rising out and up though the clouds from your plane window.

I was there before the late 2008 global financial crisis had hit Dubai; consequently there was a high level of optimism. This is a country where 80% of the population is migrant labour, meaning outsiders massively outnumber the indigenous population. The Emiraties I spoke to had mild concerns about this expressing the feeling of being 'strangers in our own country'. It is also very strange to be walking around hotels in a business suit where there are hordes of casually dressed tourists heading for the indoor ski slope at the Emirates Mall or flocking to view massive shark-infested aquariums and modern souks built in faux- traditional style.

A lovely place to have lunch but not to do business

Paris and Valbonne, France

I love the great food, lovely country roads and villages, beautiful architecture and people who I have always found to be warm, welcoming and pleasantly rude!

Unfortunately, it is just near on impossible to sell there unless the goods you are marketing are French made and you can speak French. In fact it is preferable that you *are* French. Oh, and you should employ a decent sized French workforce and work with totally French partners. So not much to ask for from a US-based company.

Business, pleasure and a typhoon
Hong Kong, China

In Hong Kong, reunified with China since 1997, there are still the English pubs, trams, high street shops that you are familiar with in London and the Hong Kong Cricket Club. So it's easy to think things haven't changed. This might be true for tourism but not for commerce. It has become increasingly important when doing business here to be able to have a local presence and Chinese language support. No longer is being Western or having the English language capability enough. You sell and market here as you do in Beijing or Shanghai.

I had just spent a week working in Beijing and was heading off to Hong Kong on a Saturday to spend the weekend seeing friends and relaxing, before meetings the following week. It is a relatively short three-hour flight to Hong Kong and – joy of joys! – I was upgraded to Business Class.

I boarded the plane and took my seat next to a short but rather rotund gentleman, who had just received a bright red cocktail drink that was placed precariously on a tray between us. I was worried about knocking his drink over and, of course, as I struggled to extricate one half of my seat belt from under his rather large behind, the drink went all over the floor and spattered across his white chino trousers. The cabin crew were quick to clean up the mess on the floor but I got a growl in response to my apology from my fellow traveller.

Two and a half hours later, we were approaching Hong Kong airport when it was obvious something was up. The sky turned black outside and there were high winds buffeting the plane. The pilot announced we were heading into a typhoon.

The two cool looking American guys on the far side of the aisle ordered two bottles of champagne and tightened their seat belts. The first approach was aborted at 180 feet above the ground and the Airbus's engines screamed as we accelerated back and up into the darkness. The cocktail-splattered gentleman next to me spoke to me for the first time. "My wife told me not to fly today, she had dreamt I was in a plane crash." "Well thanks a lot," I said and we smiled, ordered champagne with the Americans and waited for the pilot to tell us his next moves.

At the second attempt, the plane was even lower and as we aborted another landing, its engines screamed again and made loud bangs as we accelerated up through the typhoon. The noise coming from the engines was incredible. I looked across at a young female stewardess strapped in her seat across from me; tears were running down her face.

The Hong Kong airport controllers decided it was too windy to land and we were diverted into the Chinese mainland. It took an hour to reach a small Chinese city airport where we landed safely. During which time, my new best friend next to me, the two Americans (who turned out to be ex-rock band roadies and now buyers for a US-based shopping channel) and a man who had run down the plane to complain, but then saw us drinking champagne and joined in – had managed to drink the plane's entire stock of champagne.

We were transferred to a hotel, which took hours, and it was eight in the evening when we finally checked in. We had been travelling since midday. That evening the hotel was hosting a Miss China Pop Idol heat for their region and my new best friends and I had a fantastic party. At one stage, although this bit is a trifle vague, one of the Americans appeared on stage playing guitar with a Chinese 'boy band'.

Later in the afternoon of the next day we took off and landed uneventfully at Hong Kong airport. As we prepared to leave the plane one of the Americans lent over and pushed something into my hand. "Hey pal," he said, "you were great fun and in honour and memory of this flight I want you to have one of these." I looked into my hand and there was a shiny new silver dollar. "We always carry a few of these," he explained, "they go down well with the dignitaries."

Great end to a mad travelling weekend.

Peace and the temple

Taipei, Taiwan

This was my first trip to Taiwan and on the drive in from the airport it became clear that the country still has a large and vibrant manufacturing base. Coming from a country where manufacturing has more or less disappeared, it was amazing to see this vast industrial landscape. There seemed to be factories in abundance, but not much in the way of town planning. I saw high-rise residential apartment blocks sitting alongside smoke-billowing industrial complexes and multi-lane freeways. I saw a shopping mall fitting snugly between a power station and a festering polluted lake.

I had allocated a full day to an executive review with our major partner in Taipei. The meeting was formal and involved presentations from both sides. The atmosphere was very like the one I experienced in Beijing, polite but firm. The meeting concluded at lunchtime and, as seems common in this part of the world, we did not lunch together. However, one of the partner's executives took me into an ante-room for tea.

He asked me how long I was in Taipei and I said, "Just this afternoon". He then asked me if I wanted to improve my business luck in the region. "Of course," I replied. He said, "Then you need to go to Hsingtien Temple". He explained that this particular temple is dedicated to a famous general, Kuan Kung; a man who valued loyalty and righteousness above all things. Since he was adept at managing finances too, he is also worshipped as the patron saint of businessmen. "Perfect!" I thought.

Upon reaching the temple later that afternoon, I was struck by the amount of poor people begging around

the area. I gathered this was due to the number of rich businessmen visiting the temple. There were many fortune-telling stalls in an underground passageway that ran under the road opposite the temple.

It had started raining and inside the temple complex the rain mixing with the incense smoke created a very heady and pungent atmosphere. I settled into a small, sheltered corner of the temple and with my camera cradled in my arms promptly fell asleep.

Shortly after, I was awoken by a hand on my shoulder. I looked up and an elderly man stood there smiling at me. "I have noticed you have been asleep some time and I thought I would wake you before the crowds come," he said. "It's a very special place and you may want to take some pictures while it is peaceful." He turned around and started reading his prayer book and I lifted the camera to my eye.

The Basque connection

Madrid and San Sebastian, Spain

I discovered, much to my pleasure, that our Spanish business partner was founded by Basques and they have two main offices: one in Madrid and one in San Sebastian. Both cities are a culinary delight and although very different in size, nature and politics, they both have nightlife to savour.

As for doing business in Spain, a number of factors are important. First, you require a lot of patience. You must also possess a decent appreciation of food and wine. This is particularly easy in the Basque region, which lays a justifiable claim to the best food and wine in Spain. You must understand that nobody really knows what is going on and even if they do know, they may not tell you. It also helps to get emotional from time to time. It works for them.

I travelled to Madrid and San Sebastian to meet with our partner. In San Sebastian, I always have the best of times on my business travels. On this occasion I stayed in an old traditional hotel on the seafront and for the first time, between meetings, I could relax with my camera and just enjoy watching and delighting in a wonderful town going about its business and daily rituals. In Madrid, where it's more formal, we had late dinners and afterwards, I would walk off the excess by window shopping in the area around my hotel, enjoying the warm Madrid air.

Designer frenzy

Milan, Italy

In terms of my business proposition, working in Italy is similar in many ways to working in Spain. First, you have to develop a network of business partners on a regional basis, even if you are reselling to a major nationwide enterprise. The regional factor means a plethora of smaller business partners rather than the larger organisations we can recruit in Northern Europe. Consequently, having patience is a virtue when dealing with smaller organisations that have limited resources and need extra help in understanding your products and solutions.

I plied my trade in the industrial city of Milan where a decent wardrobe helps. I once sat in a Milanese restaurant, dressed in what I thought was the height of fashion, whilst a teenage dandy attired in Junior Prada seated at the next table looked me up and down and quite obviously thought I was a complete fashion disaster. Even the police look amazing in Milan, dressed in Armani designed uniforms, astride motor bikes or seated in Alfa Romeos.

The joy of Southern European countries is that despite having the ubiquitous shopping malls, there are still many small shops and restaurants. You can browse the shops on the main street as the sun goes down and then sit at an alfresco cafe, people-watching whilst you savour a drink and the rich nightlife around you.

It seemed like a good idea at the time
Reykjavik, Iceland

It seemed like a good idea to do business in Iceland back in January 2008. The country was punching above its weight, the banks seemed to be generating loads of cash by offering internet-based, high interest rate accounts, while many financial institutions invested vast amounts overseas. The country was booming, the young were in charge and it had been voted the 'coolest' place in the world. It sounded too good to be true. It was.

We had contacts with one major partner in Iceland and if we could get an agreement signed and in place, we would be the first company in the country with our particular business proposition. Once we had signed the agreement with the Icelandic partner, we had high hopes for future business. Of course this was dashed to the ground, at least for the time being, as the global financial crisis hit, the government collapsed and the banks were nationalised.

Aside from business troubles, I enjoyed visiting Iceland during the winter months. The people are interesting; their attitude is stoic and humorous. There are stunning landscapes and an abundance of space. I was lucky that even in mid-winter we managed to get out of Reykjavik, visiting coastal ports in blizzards and plunging into the steaming Blue Lagoon thermal pools in -6 degree Celsius temperatures and snowstorms.

A quick visit
Lausanne, Switzerland

My company has an office in Geneva and therefore I was a frequent visitor during 2008. We also have a business partner based in Lausanne, so happily I could fly straight to Geneva and board a train at the airport direct to Lausanne.

After the meetings I would take the train back from the picturesque Lausanne Station to Geneva. Then in the late afternoon I would fly home. So I would fly there and back in a day with less commuter stress, and sometimes quicker, then getting the tube to my London-based office across town from home.

Home base
New Jersey, USA

My biggest partner is a major telecommunications enterprise based in the United States. Their vast headquarters, referred to as campuses as an indication of their size, are an old corporate legacy from the past. A magnificent art deco figure that used to adorn the top of their old New York HQ has been relocated to their new modern offices. It stands in stark contrast against the sleek low rise office block surrounding it.

JACK DELMONTE PRINTS ARE AVAILABLE FROM TEDLEMON.COM

FRONTISPIECE: ESP001

OPPOSITE: CHN001

PAGE 6: DUB001

PAGE 8: USA001

PAGE 10: USA002

PAGE 11: USA003

PAGE 12: BRA001

PAGE 13: BRA002

PAGE 15: ARG001

PAGE 16: ARG002

PAGE 17: ARG003

PAGE 19: CHI001

PAGE 20: MEX001

PAGE 21: MEX002

PAGE 22: AUS001

PAGE 23: AUS002

PAGE 24: AUS003

PAGE 25: AUS004

PAGE 26: CHN002

PAGE 27: CHN003

PAGE 28: CHN004

PAGE 29: CHN005

PAGE 30: DUB002

PAGE 31: DUB003

PAGE 32: FRA001

PAGE 33: FRA002

PAGE 34: FRA003

PAGE 35: FRA004

PAGE 36: CHN006

PAGE 37: CHN007

PAGE 38: CHN008

PAGE 39: CHN009

PAGE 40: CHN010

PAGE 41: CHN011

PAGE 42: CHN012

PAGE 43: CHN013

PAGE 44: TAI001

PAGE 45: TAI002

PAGE 46: TAI003

PAGE 47: TAI004

PAGE 48: ESP002

PAGE 49: ESP003

PAGE 50: ESP004

PAGE 51: ESP005

PAGE 52: ESP006

PAGE 52: ESP007

PAGE 53: ESP008

PAGE 55: ITA001

PAGE 56: ICE001

PAGE 57: ICE002

PAGE 58: ICE003

PAGE 59: ICE004

PAGE 60: SWI001

PAGE 60: SWI002

PAGE 61: SWI003

PAGE 62: USA004

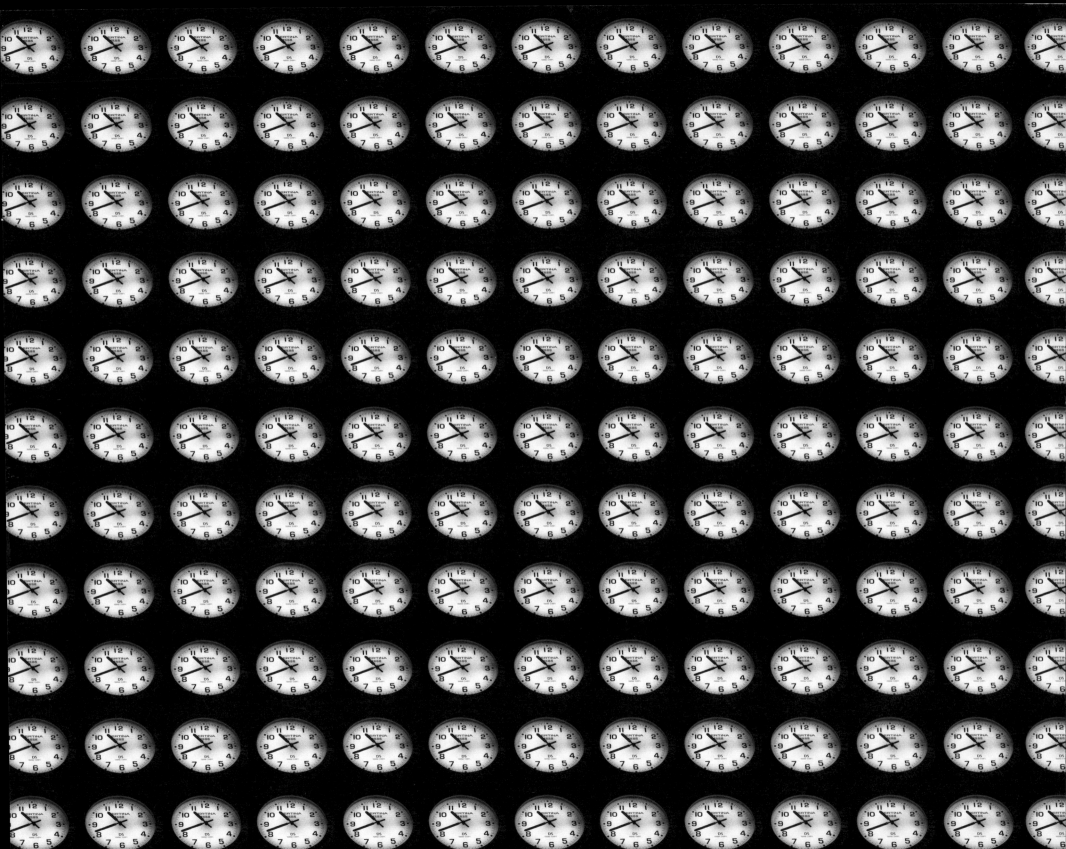